Secrets Every

Mother Should Tell
Her Daughter About

Life!

Journal

Dr. Mattie Nottage

Secrets Every Mother Should Tell Her Daughter About Life JOURNAL
by Mattie M. Nottage

Printed in the United States of America
ISBN-13: 978-0-9896003-4-7

*D*edicated to...

... my dearest daughters Magyn, Melissa, Sam, Deandra, Dearyl, *my Girls of Excellence Program*, *Faith Village For Girls Transformation & Empowerment Initiative* and the long list of beautiful women who call me "Mother."

#MOTHERSSECRETS

*T*his is the companion journal

to the "must-read" book
*"Secrets Every Mother
Should Tell Her Daughter
About Life!"*

This journal is a personal tool which allows
you to freely express your thoughts,
impressions and aspirations while reading
the life-changing book.

Journaling your own personal secrets
(footnotes) will help you to commit these
valuable nuggets to memory by expanding
your knowledge and hopefully, one day
your personal notes will be passed on to
another special, young lady.

Happy Journaling … make every day count!

With Love,
Dr. Mattie Nottage

*F*or I know the thoughts *and* plans that I have for you, says the Lord, thoughts *and* plans for welfare *and* peace and not for evil, to give you hope and a great end.

(Jeremiah 29:11)

To My Precious, Darling Daughter ...

Name:_____

_____

_____

_____

_____

_____

_____

_____

_____

_____

_____

From Your Mom, _____

Date: _____

For Secret Jottings ...

*S*ecret #1

#STAYTRUE

I will praise thee; for I am fearfully and wonderfully made ... **- Psalm 139:14**

*S*ecret #2

#THEPATHWAYOFSUCCESS

_____

_____

_____

_____

_____

_____

_____

_____

_____

_____

_____

_____

_____

I press towards the mark for the prize of the high
calling of God in Christ Jesus. – **Philippians 3:14**

Secret #3

#KEEPYOURHEARTPURE

Keep thy heart with all diligence; for out of it are the issues of life. – **Proverbs 4:23**

$\mathscr{S}$ecret #4

#RELATIONSHIPS

_____

_____

_____

_____

_____

_____

_____

_____

_____

_____

_____

_____

_____

_____

_____

"... get to know those who labor among you recognize
them for what they are, acknowledge and appreciate
and respect them all] ..." **- 1 Thessalonians 5:12**

*S*ecret #5

#BEAUTYINSIDE

_____

_____

_____

_____

_____

_____

_____

_____

_____

_____

_____

_____

_____

Thou are all fair (beautiful), my love; there is no spot in thee. – **Song of Solomon 4:7**

Secret #6

#ENJOYYOURMOMENTS

And he shall be like a tree planted by the rivers of water, that bringeth forth his fruit in his season; his leaf also shall not wither; and whatsoever he doeth shall prosper.– **Psalm 1:3**

*S*ecret #7

#PRICELESS

But [you] are a chosen generation, a royal
priesthood, an holy nation, a peculiar people...
- 1 Peter 2:9

*S*ecret #8

#ABSOLUTELYSURE

_____

_____

_____

_____

_____

_____

_____

_____

_____

_____

_____

_____

_____

_____

And the Lord God said, ... I will make him an help meet (suitable) for him. - **Genesis 2:18**

Secret #9

#SEIZEOPPORTUNITIES

_____

_____

_____

_____

_____

_____

_____

_____

_____

_____

_____

_____

_____

_____

Making the very most of the time [buying up each opportunity], because the days are evil.–
Ephesians 5:16 AMP

$\mathscr{S}$ecret #10
#PROCRASTINATION

_____

_____

_____

_____

_____

_____

_____

_____

_____

_____

_____

_____

_____

_____

Ye a little sleep, a little slumber, a little folding of
the hands to sleep: So shall thy poverty come ... as
an armed man. – **Proverbs 6:10, 11**

*S*ecret #11

#NOTICEOPPORTUNITIES

_____

_____

_____

_____

_____

_____

_____

_____

_____

_____

_____

_____

_____

_____

Behave yourselves wisely [living prudently and with discretion] ... making the very most of the time *and* seizing ... the opportunity. -**Colossians 4:5**

$\mathscr{S}$ecret #12

#MAKEGOOD

_____

_____

_____

_____

_____

_____

_____

_____

_____

_____

_____

_____

_____

... now is the acceptable time ... making the very most of the time [buying up each opportunity]...
- **2 Corinthians 6:2a; Ephesians 5:16a**

*S*ecret #13

#SAVEYOURSELF4MARRIAGE

_____

_____

_____

_____

_____

_____

_____

_____

_____

_____

_____

_____

_____

_____

For this is the will of God, your sanctification: that
you abstain from sexual immorality; fornication.
– 1 Thessalonians 4:3

Secret #14

#JUSTDOIT!

_____

_____

_____

_____

_____

_____

_____

_____

_____

_____

_____

_____

_____

_____

"Nevertheless at thy word, I will..."
- Luke 5:5

*S*ecret #15

#DONOTWASTETIME

See then that you walk circumspectly, not as fools
but wise, redeeming the time... **Ephesians 5:15-16**

Secret #16

#DONTLOWERTHESTANDARD

Nevertheless, [to avoid] fornication, let every man
have his own wife, and let every woman have her
own husband. – **1 Corinthians 7:2**

$\mathscr{S}$ecret #17

#DONOTBEMISLED

Do not be deceived: "Bad company corrupts good morals. **- 1 Corinthians 15:33**

*S*ecret #18

#SEEKGOD

Delight thyself also in the LORD; and he shall give
thee the desires of thine heart. – **Proverbs 37:4**

Secret #19

#DEDICATIONTOGOD

Commit thy works unto the Lord and the thoughts shall be established. – **Proverbs 16:3**

Secret #20

#LOVE

Jesus said unto him, "Thou shalt love the Lord thy God with all thy heart and with all thy soul, and with all thy mind. – **Matthew 22:37**

*S*ecret #21

#NEVERFORGET

" ... love covers a multitude of sins [forgives and
disregards the offenses of others]."
– 1 Peter 4:8

$\mathscr{S}$ecret #22

#RELEASEPEOPLE

_____

_____

_____

_____

_____

_____

_____

_____

_____

_____

_____

_____

As for a man who stirs up division, after warning him once and then twice, have nothing more to do with him .... **– Titus 3:1**

$\mathscr{S}$ecret #23

#WALKAWAYFROMABUSE

As for a man who stirs up division, after warning
him once and then twice, have nothing more to do
with him …. **– Titus 3:10**

*S*ecret #24

#CHANGE4PROGRESS

_____

_____

_____

_____

_____

_____

_____

_____

_____

_____

_____

_____

_____

_____

_____

... be ye transformed by the renewing of your mind... - **Romans 12:2**

*S*ecret #25

#PERSONALINDEPENDENCE

A good woman is hard to find, and worth far more
than diamonds. - **Proverbs 31:10**

$\mathscr{S}$ecret #26

#ADVERSESITUATIONS

And we know that all things work together for good
to them that love God .... – **Romans 8:28**

$\mathscr{S}$ecret #27

#3WPURPOSEFACTORS

By having the eyes of your understanding
enlightened, you can know and understand the
hope to which He has called you...
– Ephesians 1:18

Secret #28

#USEOPPOSITION

For I consider that the sufferings of the present time (present life) are not worth being compared with the glory that is about to be revealed to us.
– Romans 8:18

Secret #29

#GETBACKINTHEFIGHT

And let us not grow weary of doing good, for in due season we will reap, if we do not give up.
– **Galatians 6:9**

$\mathscr{S}$ecret #30

#CROSSWINDS

Be ye steadfast, unmovable, always abounding in the work of the Lord ... – **1 Corinthians 15:58**

$\mathscr{S}$ecret #31

#CELEBRATEWOMANHOOD

_____

_____

_____

_____

_____

_____

_____

_____

_____

_____

_____

_____

_____

You made all the delicate, inner parts of my body
and knit me together in my mother's womb.
– Psalm 139:13

𝒮ecret #32

#BYGODSGRACE

_____

_____

_____

_____

_____

_____

_____

_____

_____

_____

_____

_____

_____

By the grace (the unmerited favor and blessing) of God I am what I am …. – **1 Corinthians 15:10**

$\mathcal{S}$ecret #33

#SELFANALYSIS

Let every person carefully scrutinize and examine
and test his own conduct and his own work.
– Galatians 6:4

Secret #34

#TAKINGADVICE

The way of fools seems right to them, but the wise
listen to godly advice. – **Proverbs 12:15**

*S*ecret #35

#YOURNUMBER1FAN

_____

_____

_____

_____

_____

_____

_____

_____

_____

_____

_____

_____

_____

_____

_____

_____

...but David encouraged himself in the LORD his
God... - **1 Samuel 30:6**

Secret #36

#KEEPDANCING

_____

_____

_____

_____

_____

_____

_____

_____

_____

_____

_____

_____

_____

Then shall the young women rejoice in the dance ...
Jeremiah 31:13

$\mathscr{S}$ecret #37

#DONOTSETTLE

... No, ... but I will buy it of you for a price. I will not offer burnt offerings to the Lord my God of that which costs me nothing ... **2 Samuel 24:24**

$\mathscr{S}$ecret #38

#NEVERCOMPROMISE

Your gift will make room for you and set you before great men. - **Proverbs 18:16**

Secret #39

#WORTHANDVALUE

_____

_____

_____

_____

_____

_____

_____

_____

_____

_____

_____

_____

_____

_____

[Be] not slothful in business; fervent in spirit;
– Romans. 12:11

$\mathscr{S}$ecret #40

#PAMPERYOURSELF

_____

_____

_____

_____

_____

_____

_____

_____

_____

_____

_____

_____

_____

And He said to them, "Come away by yourselves to a lonely place and rest a while." - **Mark 6:3**

Secret #41

#YOUAREANEAGLE

"But they that wait upon the LORD shall renew their
strength; they shall mount up with wings as
eagles; …" - **Isaiah 40:31**

$\mathscr{S}$ecret #42

#PERSONALPRUDENCE

"I, Wisdom ... make prudence my dwelling ...
– Proverbs 8:12

*S*ecret #43

#PATIENCEVIRTUEPOWER

_____

_____

_____

_____

_____

_____

_____

_____

_____

_____

_____

_____

_____

But let patience have her perfect work, that ye may
be perfect and entire, wanting nothing. **– James 1:4**

$\mathscr{S}$ecret #44

#PERSEVERANCE

_____

_____

_____

_____

_____

_____

_____

_____

_____

_____

_____

_____

_____

"For the vision is yet for an appointed time,...:
though it tarry, wait for it; because it will surely
come, it will not tarry."   **- Habakkuk. 2:3**

*S*ecret #45

#GETYOURGOLD

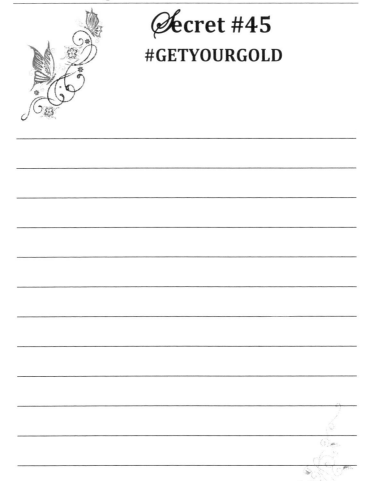

Set your affection on things above, not on things on the earth. - **Colossians 3:2**

Secret #46

#FOCUSONYOURFUTURE

_...forgetting those things which are behind, and
reaching forth unto those things which are before..._
– Philippians. 3:13

*S*ecret #47

#GREATEXPECTATION

_____

_____

_____

_____

_____

_____

_____

_____

_____

_____

_____

_____

_____

Forget the former things; do not dwell on the past.
See I am doing a new thing!
Isaiah 43:18-19

*S*ecret #48

#YOURDESTINY

_____

_____

_____

_____

_____

_____

_____

_____

_____

_____

_____

_____

_____

_____

_____

"For the vision [is] yet for an appointed time, but at the end it shall speak, and not lie..."
- **Habbakuk 2:3**

Secret #49

#PASTPRESENTFUTURE

Grace be unto you, and peace, from him which is,
and which was, and which is to come …
– Revelation 1:4

Secret #50

#GLEANFROMOTHERS

A wise [person] will hear, and will increase learning; and a person of understanding shall attain unto wise counsels: - **Proverbs 1:5**

$\mathscr{S}$ecret #51

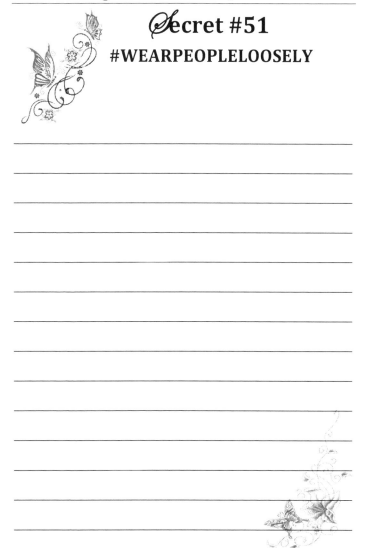

#WEARPEOPLELOOSELY

_____

_____

_____

_____

_____

_____

_____

_____

_____

_____

_____

_____

_____

_____

Put not your trust in princes, nor in the son of
man, .. – **Psalm 146**

$\mathscr{S}$ecret #52

#WHATYOUBECOME

_____

_____

_____

_____

_____

_____

_____

_____

_____

_____

_____

_____

_____

_____

Therefore if anyone is in Christ he is a new creation. The old has passed away; the new has come. **- 2 Corinthians. 5:1**

*S*ecret #53

#TRUSTGOD

Trust in the Lord with ALL your heart and lean not to your own understanding. – **Proverbs 3:5**

$\mathscr{S}$ecret #54

#LOVEANDINTEGRITY

_____

_____

_____

_____

_____

_____

_____

_____

_____

_____

_____

_____

_____

... neither cast ye your **pearls before swine**, lest they trample them under their feet, and turn again and rend you.   – **Matthew 7:6**

$\mathscr{S}$ecret #55

#LEARNFROMOTHERS

_____

_____

_____

_____

_____

_____

_____

_____

_____

_____

_____

_____

_____

_____

_____

These things happened to them as examples and
were written down as warnings for us...
– 1 Corinthians 10:11

Secret #56

#SEEGOODANDBADINALL

_____

_____

_____

_____

_____

_____

_____

_____

_____

_____

_____

_____

_____

_____

Wherefore by their fruits ye shall know them.
– Matthew 7:20

Secret #57

#MAXIMIZEYOURNOW

_____

_____

_____

_____

_____

_____

_____

_____

_____

_____

_____

_____

_____

The righteous keep moving forward, and those with
clean hands become stronger and stronger.
- Job 17:9

*S*ecret #58

#PEOPLEWILLLISTEN

A word fitly spoken is like apples of gold in pictures
of silver. – **Proverbs 25:11**

*S*ecret #59

#DONOTWASTEWORDS

Fools find no pleasure in understanding, but delight
in airing their own opinions. – **Proverbs 18:2**

*S*ecret #60

#PUSHTOWARDSDESTINY

He that walketh with wise men shall be wise: but a companion of fools shall be destroyed
- **Proverbs 13:20**

*S*ecret #61

#DREAMSVISIONSIDEAS

_____

_____

_____

_____

_____

_____

_____

_____

_____

_____

_____

_____

_____

_____

For I know the thoughts *and* plans that I have for you, says the Lord **Jeremiah 29:11 AMP**

*S*ecret #62

#READTHEFINEPRINT

And in all your getting, get understanding.
Proverbs 4:7

Secret #63

#THEBETTERYOU

_____

_____

_____

_____

_____

_____

_____

_____

_____

_____

_____

_____

_____

The LORD will perfect that which concerns me...
- Psalm 138:8

*S*ecret #64

#LEAVEAGOODMEMORY

The memory of the just is blessed...
- **Proverbs 10:7**

*S*ecret #65

#HARDWORK

_____

_____

_____

_____

_____

_____

_____

_____

_____

_____

_____

_____

_____

I must work the works of him that sent me, while it
is day: the night cometh, when no man can work.
John 9:4

*S*ecret #66

#PRINCIPLESABOUTDOORS

See, I have placed before you an open door that no
one can shut. **- Revelations 3:8**

$\mathcal{S}$ecret #67

#MORALSANDPRINCIPLES

_____

_____

_____

_____

_____

_____

_____

_____

_____

_____

_____

_____

_____

But when He, the Spirit of Truth (the Truth-giving Spirit) comes, He will guide you into all the Truth (the whole, full Truth.)- **John 16:13**

$\mathscr{S}$ecret #68

#GODLYSTANDARDS

All scripture is given by inspiration of God, and is profitable for doctrine, for reproof, for correction, for instruction in righteousness: – **2 Timothy 3:16**

Secret #69

#SMILEANYWAY

In everything give thanks: for this is the will of God in Christ Jesus concerning you.
– 1 Thessalonians 5:18

Secret #70

#INTEGRITY

The integrity of the upright shall guide them: but the perverseness of transgressors shall destroy them. - **Proverbs 11:3**

*S*ecret #71

#OUTSTANDINGINTEGRITY

The just walketh in integrity: their children [are] blessed after them. – **Proverbs 20:7**

Secret #72

#BETRUE

_____

_____

_____

_____

_____

_____

_____

_____

_____

_____

_____

_____

_____

_____

Provide things honest in the sight of all men.
– Romans 12:17

*S*ecret #73

#ALWAYSHELP

...It is more blessed to give than to receive
-    **Acts 20:35**

*S*ecret #74

#KNOWLEDGE#WISDOM #UNDERSTANDING

...Therefore get wisdom, and with all your getting get understanding... - **Proverbs 4:7**

Secret #75

#KNOWLEDGEBUILDS
#WISDOMBEAUTIFIES

Wisdom builds her house...
Proverbs 14:1

$\mathscr{S}$ecret #76

#APPLYINFORMATION

Wisdom is better than strength: ...
Ecclesiastes 9:16

$\mathcal{S}$ecret #77
#COUNTYOURMONEY

_____

_____

_____

_____

_____

_____

_____

_____

_____

_____

_____

_____

_____

For which of you, intending to build a tower, sitteth not down first, and counteth the cost, whether he have sufficient to finish it? – **Luke 14:28**

$\mathscr{S}$ecret #78

#SAVEANDINVEST

_____

_____

_____

_____

_____

_____

_____

_____

_____

_____

_____

_____

_____

Cast your bread upon the waters for you will find it after many days. – **Ecclesiastes 11:1**

Secret #79

#ALWAYSRESPECTTIME

_____

_____

_____

_____

_____

_____

_____

_____

_____

_____

_____

_____

_____

_____

_____

To every season there is a purpose and a time for
everything under the heavens ... **- Ecclesiastes. 3:1**

*S*ecret #80

#DONTLETPEOPLEDUMPONYOU

A good man out of the good treasure of his heart
brings forth good; For out of the abundance of the
heart his mouth speak. **- Luke 6:45**

Secret #81

#JUSTPRAY

"Therefore, confess your sins to one another and pray for one another ..." – **James 5:16**

Secret #82

#LETPEOPLELEARN

Cast thy burden upon the LORD, and he shall sustain thee: he shall never suffer the righteous to be moved.
– Proverbs 55:22

*S*ecret #83

#NEVERSAYICANT

_____

_____

_____

_____

_____

_____

_____

_____

_____

_____

_____

_____

_____

_____

I can do all things through Jesus Christ who
strengthens me. - **Philippians 4:13**

*S*ecret #84

#GUARDYOURHEART

Keep (guard) your heart with all diligence for out of it flows the issues of life. – **Proverbs 4:2**

*S*ecret #85

#WAITONLOVE

Wait on the Lord and be of good courage and he shall strengthen thine heart; wait I say on the Lord.
Psalm 27:14

Secret #86

#SYMPATHYVSEMPATHY

_____

_____

_____

_____

_____

_____

_____

_____

_____

_____

_____

_____

_____

_____

_____

This is my commandment, That ye love one another, as I have loved you. – **John 15:12**

*S*ecret #87

#DONTSTEALORBORROW

The rich rule over the poor; and the borrower is
slave to the lender. **Proverbs 22:7**

Secret #88

#ABIRDINTHEHANDISBETTER

He is a rewarder of those who diligently seek Him.
Hebrews 11:6

$\mathcal{S}$ecret #89

#YOURSEASONOFDOUBLE

Instead of shame you will receive a double portion
...You will inherit a double portion in your land and
everlasting joy will be yours. – **Isaiah 61:7, 8**

Secret #90

#CHANGEISNECESSARY

... after that ye have suffered a while, he will perfect,
establish, strengthen, and settle you. - **1 Peter 5:10**

Secret #91

#RESPECTISEARNED

_____

_____

_____

_____

_____

_____

_____

_____

_____

_____

_____

_____

_____

_____

_____

Therefore all things whatsoever ye would that men
should do to you, do you even so to them:
Matthew 7:12

*S*ecret #92

#THEWISDOMPRINCIPLE

Wisdom is the principle thing.
– Proverbs 4:7

*S*ecret #93

#MAKETHEJOURNEY

Let us lay aside every weight, and the sin which doth so easily beset us, and let us run with patience the race that is set before us. - **Hebrews 12:1**

*S*ecret #94

#LEARNWHENTOSAYNO

_____

_____

_____

_____

_____

_____

_____

_____

_____

_____

_____

_____

_____

"I am saying this for your own good, not to restrict you,
but that you may live in a right way in undivided
devotion to the Lord." - **1 Corinthians 7:35**

Secret #95

#DISCIPLINEISPRIORITY

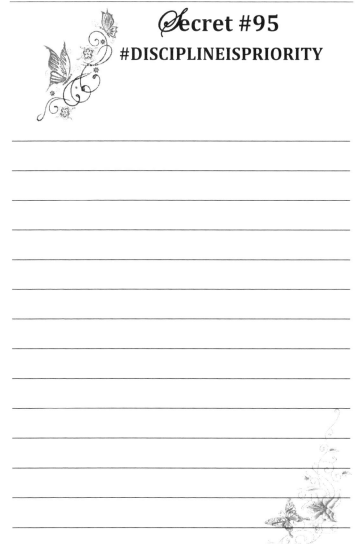

_____

_____

_____

_____

_____

_____

_____

_____

_____

_____

_____

_____

_____

_____

"He that [hath] no rule over his own spirit [is like] a
city [that is] broken down, [and] without walls."
Proverbs 25:28

*S*ecret #96

#STAYSOBER

Be sober, be vigilant; because[a] your adversary
the devil walks about like a roaring lion, seeking
whom he may devour. - **1 Peter 5:8**

Secret #97

#THEPATHWAYOFSUCCESS

...teach the young women to be **S.O.B.E.R**...
– Titus 2:4

Secret #98

#FOCUSONYOURDESTINY

...if therefore thine eye be single, thy whole body shall be full of light. **– Matthew 6:22**

Secret #99

#MODERATION

A false balance is abomination to the Lord: ...
Proverbs 11:1

*S*ecret #100

#PEOPLEARESHIFTY

_____

_____

_____

_____

_____

_____

_____

_____

_____

_____

_____

_____

_____

Do not trust a neighbor; put no confidence in a
friend; wait for God your Savior; your God will hear
you. – **Micah 7:5, 7**

*S*ecret #101

#DELAYISNOTDENIAL

_____

_____

_____

_____

_____

_____

_____

_____

_____

_____

_____

_____

_____

For yet a little while, and He that shall come; will come and will not tarry. **- Hebrews 10:37**

Secret #102
#KEEPYOURAREACLEAN

_____

_____

_____

_____

_____

_____

_____

_____

_____

_____

_____

_____

_____

_____

The wise woman builds her house...
– Proverbs 14:1

*S*ecret #103

#MAKEOTHERSRESPONSIBLE

Wherefore comfort yourselves together, and edify
one another... **- 1 Thessalonians. 5:11**

*S*ecret #104

#TAKERESPONSIBILITY

_____

_____

_____

_____

_____

_____

_____

_____

_____

_____

_____

_____

_____

_____

For every man shall bear his own burden.

- **Galatians 6:5**

Secret #105
#FORGIVEQUICKLY

_____

_____

_____

_____

_____

_____

_____

_____

_____

_____

_____

_____

_____

And when ye stand praying, forgive, if ye have ought against any: that your Father also which is in heaven may forgive you your trespasses. - **Mark 11:25**

Secret #106
#CHANGEISCONSTANT

_____

_____

_____

_____

_____

_____

_____

_____

_____

_____

_____

_____

_____

_____

"For I the LORD do not change..."
- Malachi 3:6

*S*ecret #107

#NEVERBELIEVEALIE

Then you will know the truth, and the truth will set you free. – **John 8:32**

Secret #108
#MAKETHINGSHAPPEN

_____

_____

_____

_____

_____

_____

_____

_____

_____

_____

_____

_____

_____

_____

_____

And I say unto you, Ask, and it shall be given you; seek, and ye shall find; knock, and it shall be opened unto you. - **Matthew 7:7**

*S*ecret #109

#DONTSETTLEFORORDINARY

But we have this treasure in earthen vessels, that the excellency of the power may be of God, and not of us. – **2 Corinthians 4:7**

Secret #110

#GODMADEYOUDIFFERENT

Being confident of this very thing, that he which
hath begun a good work in you will perform [it]
until the day of Jesus Christ. – **Philippians 1:6**

*S*ecret #111

#ACCEPTYOURSELF

_____

_____

_____

_____

_____

_____

_____

_____

_____

_____

_____

_____

_____

_____

_____

For we are His workmanship created in Christ unto good works . – **Ephesians 2:10**

*S*ecret #112

#DONTBAFRAID2ASK

_____

_____

_____

_____

_____

_____

_____

_____

_____

_____

_____

_____

_____

_____

_____

And shall make him of quick understanding in
the fear of the Lord: ... – **Isaiah 11:3**

Secret #113

#STAND4WHATUBELIEVE

Be alert and on your guard; Stand firm in your faith.
- **I Corinthians 16:13**

*S*ecret #114

#DONTTAKENO4ANANSWER

_____

_____

_____

_____

_____

_____

_____

_____

_____

_____

_____

_____

_____

_____

"...ask, and ye shall receive, that your joy may be full." – **John 16:24**

*S*ecret #115

#GETTHEHONEY

Many are the afflictions of the righteous: but the
LORD delivers us out of them all. – **Psalm 34:19**

Secret #116

#GODWILLLIFTYOU

_____

_____

_____

_____

_____

_____

_____

_____

_____

_____

_____

_____

_____

_____

_____

But You, O Lord, are a shield for me, my glory, and
the lifter of my head. – **Psalm 3:3**

Secret #117

#THEHAPPYHAPPYSONG

_____

_____

_____

_____

_____

_____

_____

_____

_____

_____

_____

_____

_____

_____

"My soul magnifies _and_ extols the Lord; and my
spirit rejoices in God my Savior." – **Luke 1:46-47**

*Se*cret #118

#YOURSOULSFRAGRANCE

_____

_____

_____

_____

_____

_____

_____

_____

_____

_____

_____

_____

_____

_____

Yet a time is coming and has now come when the
true worshipers will worship the Father in the
Spirit and in truth..." – **John 4:23**

Secret #119

#GODSAPPLAUSE

... for the joy of the Lord is your strength.
Nehemiah 8:10

*S*ecret #120

#PRACTICE4SUCCESS

Study to shew thyself approved unto God, a workman that needeth not to be ashamed, rightly dividing the word of truth -**2 Timothy 2:5**

*S*ecret #121
#HOW2HANDLEMISTAKES

"Though he fall, he shall not be utterly cast down:
for the LORD upholdeth him with his hand."
Psalm 37:24

*S*ecret #122

#STARTSTRONGENDSTRONG

_____

_____

_____

_____

_____

_____

_____

_____

_____

_____

_____

_____

_____

_____

"I press toward the mark of the higher calling found in Christ Jesus." **- Philippians 3:14**

*S*ecret #123

#WHEN2TELLYOURSTORY

_____

_____

_____

_____

_____

_____

_____

_____

_____

_____

_____

_____

_____

_____

And they overcame him by the blood of the lamb
and by the word of my testimony
Revelations 12:11

*S*ecret #124

#MAKESOMEONESLIFEBETTER

_____

_____

_____

_____

_____

_____

_____

_____

_____

_____

_____

_____

_____

[No] you yourselves are our letter of recommendation ... written in your hearts, to be known ... and read by everybody. - **2 Corinthians 3:2(AMP)**

*S*ecret #125

#GETTINGTHEBESTRESULTS

"You will seek me and find me when you seek me
with all your heart." - **Jeremiah 29:13**

$\mathscr{S}$ecret #126

#AVOIDSHORTCUTS

_____

_____

_____

_____

_____

_____

_____

_____

_____

_____

_____

_____

_____

Enter through the narrow gate. For wide is the gate
and broad is the road that leads to destruction, and
many enter through it.   - **Matthew 7:13**

$\mathscr{S}$ecret #127

#STARTINGOVER

... his mercies never come to an end; they are new
every morning; - **Lamentations 3:22**

*S*ecret #128

#STARTINGOVERAGAIN

_____

_____

_____

_____

_____

_____

_____

_____

_____

_____

_____

_____

_____

_____

_____

But grow in the grace and knowledge of our Lord and Savior Jesus Christ. - **2 Peter 3:18**

Secret #129

#THECALCULATEDRISK

Invest in seven ventures, yes, in eight; you do not know what disaster may come upon the land.

Ecclesiastes 11:2

*S*ecret #130

#SPEAKUP4YOURSELF

...and [be] ready always to [give] an answer to every man that ask you a reason of the hope that is in you ... – **1 Peter 3:15-16**

$\mathscr{S}$ecret #131

#FINDAWAYOUT

...but with the temptation [God] will also make a
way to escape, that ye may be able to bear it.
– 1 Corinthians 10:13

*S*ecret #132

#MAINTAINYOURCOMPOSURE

Cast not away therefore your confidence, which hath great recompense of reward - **Hebrews 10:35**

*S*ecret #133

#STRIVE2BTHEBEST

Let your light so shine before men, that they may
see your good works, and glorify your Father which
is in heaven. – **Matthew 5:16**

*S*ecret #134

#SETHIGHSTANDARDS

_____

_____

_____

_____

_____

_____

_____

_____

_____

_____

_____

_____

_____

_____

_____

Be thou an example of the believers, in word, in
conversation, in charity, in spirit, in faith, in purity.
– 1 Timothy 4:12

$\mathscr{S}$ecret #135

#FINDINGFAVOR

For whoso findeth me findeth life, and shall obtain
favour of the LORD. – **Proverbs 8:3**

Secret #136

#RESPECT

_____

_____

_____

_____

_____

_____

_____

_____

_____

_____

_____

_____

_____

Pay to all what is owed to them: ...respect to whom respect is owed, honor to whom honor is owed. –
Romans 13:7

*S*ecret #137
#THERIGHTATTITUDE

_____

_____

_____

_____

_____

_____

_____

_____

_____

_____

_____

_____

_____

_____

_____

Be completely humble and gentle; be patient,
bearing with one another in love. - **Ephesians 4:2**

*S*ecret #138

#ONEGOD

_____

_____

_____

_____

_____

_____

_____

_____

_____

_____

_____

_____

_____

_____

Thus saith the LORD the King of Israel, and his redeemer the LORD of hosts; I [am] the first, and I [am] the last; and beside me [there is] no God. **Isaiah 44:6**

*S*ecret #139

#HESEVERYTHINGYOUNEED

_____

_____

_____

_____

_____

_____

_____

_____

_____

_____

_____

_____

_____

But the Helper, the Holy Spirit, whom the Father
will send in My name, He will teach you all things...
– **John 14:26**

$\mathscr{S}$ecret #140

#PEACEOFGOD

_____

_____

_____

_____

_____

_____

_____

_____

_____

_____

_____

_____

_____

_____

And the peace of God, which surpasses all understanding, will guard your hearts and your minds in Christ Jesus. - **Philippians 4:7**

*S*ecret #141

#DISCOVERYANDREDISCOVERY

Before you were born, I set you apart and
appointed you ... - **Jeremiah 1:5**

Secret #142

#DISCOVERYOURSELFINGOD

But you are ...God's special possession, that you may declare the praises of him who called you out of darkness into his wonderful light. – **1 Peter 2:9**

*S*ecret #143
#LISTENINGISVITAL

_____

_____

_____

_____

_____

_____

_____

_____

_____

_____

_____

_____

_____

_____

Hear counsel, and receive instruction, that thou
mayest be wise in thy latter end.
– Proverbs 19:20

Secret #144

#THINKHIGHLYOFYOURSELF

For thus saith the LORD of hosts; for he that
toucheth you toucheth the apple of his eye.
- **Zechariah 2:8**

Secret #145

#PERPETUALJOY

_____

_____

_____

_____

_____

_____

_____

_____

_____

_____

_____

_____

_____

_____

Your heart shall rejoice, and your joy no man taketh from you." - **John 16:32**

$\mathscr{S}$ecret #146

#REMAINTRUE2YOURSELF
#REMAINTRUETOGOD

_____

_____

_____

_____

_____

_____

_____

_____

_____

_____

_____

_____

_____

_____

Be on your guard; stand firm in the faith; be
courageous; be strong. Do everything in love.
– 1 Corinthians 16:13-14

Secret #147

#MAKERIGHTCHOICES

Give careful thought to the paths for your feet and be steadfast in all your ways. - **Proverbs 4:26**

*S*ecret #148

#LEARNTOVALUETIME

_____

_____

_____

_____

_____

_____

_____

_____

_____

_____

_____

_____

_____

_____

To everything there is a season, and a time to every purpose under the heaven: - **Ecclesiastes 3:1**

Secret #149

#DONOTWASTETIME

Walk in wisdom toward them that are without,
redeeming the time. – **Colossians 4:5**

$\mathscr{S}$ecret #150

#DONTLETPEOPLEMISLEADYOU

Where no counsel is, the people fall: but in the
multitude of counselors there is safety.
Proverbs 11:14

*S*ecret #151

#THERIGHTPEOPLE

_____

_____

_____

_____

_____

_____

_____

_____

_____

_____

_____

_____

_____

_____

You use steel to sharpen steel, and one friend [in God] sharpens another. – **Proverbs 27:17**

Secret #152

#ALWAYSCONSULTGOD

_____

_____

_____

_____

_____

_____

_____

_____

_____

_____

_____

_____

_____

_____

... and whatsoever he doeth shall prosper.
Psalm 1:3

Secret #153

#ADEADENDISNOTHEEND

... I will lead them in paths they have not
known: I will make crooked paths straight before
them. – **Isaiah 42:16**

Secret #154

#DOOR2DIVINEPURPOSE

_____

_____

_____

_____

_____

_____

_____

_____

_____

_____

_____

_____

_____

_____

For every one that asketh receiveth; and he that seeketh findeth; and to him that knocketh it shall be opened. – **Matthew 7:8**

Secret #155

#GODSTILLHASAPLAN

_____

_____

_____

_____

_____

_____

_____

_____

_____

_____

_____

_____

_____

_____

Many are the plans in the mind of a man, but it is
the purpose of the LORD that will stand.
Proverbs 19:21

Secret #156

#UPGRADEYOURSTATUS

Every good and perfect gift is from above, coming
down from the Father of the heavenly lights,...
James 1:17

Secret #157

#WHATYOUSHOULDBEDOING

_____

_____

_____

_____

_____

_____

_____

_____

_____

_____

_____

_____

_____

_____

I desire to do your will, my God; your law is within my heart. - **Psalm 40:8**

*S*ecret #158

#DANCEB4HIM

_____

_____

_____

_____

_____

_____

_____

_____

_____

_____

_____

_____

_____

_____

And David danced before the Lord with all his might ...
2 Samuel 6:14

*S*ecret #159

#EMBRACINGLIFESLESSONS

Beloved, do not think it strange, the fiery trial
which is to try you, as though some strange thing
happened to you ... – **1 Peter 4:12**

𝒮ecret #160

#DOITANYWAY

_____

_____

_____

_____

_____

_____

_____

_____

_____

_____

_____

_____

_____

_____

For a great door is opened unto me, and there are
many adversaries.   **- 1 Corinthians 16:9**

$\mathscr{S}$ecret #161

#FINDINGTRUEPURPOSE

I raised you up for this very purpose, that I might display my power in you, and that my name may be proclaimed in all the earth. – **Romans 9:17**

✑ecret #162

#FINDINGYOURPURPOSE

For we are His workmanship created in Christ Jesus unto good works which God has before ordained that we should walk in them. - E**phesians. 2:10**

*S*ecret #163

#MOUNTAINTOPANOINTING

Yea, though I walk through the valley of the shadow of death, I will fear no evil ... – **Psalm 23:4**

*S*ecret #164

#KEEPYOURDREAMSALIVE

The vision is for an appointed time it shall speak
and lie not ... - **Habbakuk 2:3**

*S*ecret #165

#DIGDEEPER

In your presence there is fullness of joy at your right
hand are pleasures forever more ... you surround us
with your favor Oh Lord ... - **Psalm 16:11**

*S*ecret #166

#SOWINGANDREAPING

_____

_____

_____

_____

_____

_____

_____

_____

_____

_____

_____

_____

_____

_____

_____

For they have sown the wind, and they shall reap the whirlwind: - **Hosea 8:8**

*S*ecret #167

#ROAD2PROSPERITY

But thou shalt remember the LORD thy God: for it is he that giveth thee power to get wealth …
–Deuteronomy 8:18

$\mathscr{S}$ecret #168

#DONTSTART
#WHATYOUCANTFINISH

Be not deceived; God is not mocked: for whatsoever
a man soweth, that shall he also reap.
Galatians 6:7

$\mathscr{S}$ecret #170

#TRUSTINGGOD

Trust in the LORD with all thine heart; and lean not unto
thine own understanding ... In all thy ways acknowledge
him, and he shall direct thy paths. **Proverbs 3:5, 6**

*S*ecret #169

#DORIGHTBYOTHERS

And as ye would that men should do to you, do
ye also to them likewise. – **Luke 6:31**

My Book Of Secrets ...

_____

_____

_____

_____

_____

_____

_____

_____

_____

Signed:

_____

Order your copy today!

*"Secrets Every Mother
Should Tell Her Daughter
About Life!"*

and

*"A Mother's Book Of Prayers
For Her Daughter"*

Author of the best-selling book
*"Breaking The Chains,
From Worship To Warfare"*

Dr. Mattie Nottage
Ministry Profile

Dr. Mattie Nottage is an international motivational/inspirational speaker, teacher, preacher, prophet, life-coach, playwright, author and gospel recording artist. She co-pastors with her husband, Apostle Edison Nottage, Believers Faith Outreach Ministries, Int'l in beautiful Nassau, Bahamas.

She is the president and founder of Mattie Nottage Ministries, Int'l, The Faith Village For Girls Transformation & Empowerment Program, The Youth In Action Group and The Global Dominion Network Empowerment Group of Kingdom 500 Companies. She is the author of her best-selling book, ***"Breaking The Chains, From Worship To Warfare!"*** along with numerous other publications.

Dr. Nottage has regularly appeared as a guest on numerous television networks including, The Trinity Broadcasting Network (T.B.N.), The Word Network, Atlanta Live WATC TV 57 and so many more. Additionally, she is the host and producer of her very own impacting television and radio show, ***"Transforming Lives!"***

SECRETS Every Mother Should Tell Her Daughter About Life! JOURNAL

To request Dr. Mattie Nottage for a speaking engagement, upcoming event, life coaching seminar or mentorship sessions or to place an order for products, please contact:

Mattie Nottage Ministries, International (Bahamas Address)

P.O. Box SB-52524
Nassau, N. P. Bahamas
Tel/Fax (242) 698-1383
*Or **(954) 237-8196***

OR

Mattie Nottage Ministries, International (U.S. Address)

6511 Nova Dr., Suite #193
Davie, Florida 33317
*Tel/Fax: **(888) 825-7568***
UK Tel: 44 (0) 203371 9922

OR

www.mattienottage.org

You can follow us onYoutube, Facebook @ DrMattie Nottage and Twitter @DrMattieNottage